城市设计

How We Organize Ourselves | Non-Fiction Series

Copyright © 2022 by Level Learning, INC. and Washington Yu Ying PCS™
Original and Edited Text Copyright © 2022 by Washington Yu Ying PCS™

All rights reserved. No part of this book in whole or part may be reproduced without written permission from the publisher.

Published by Level Learning, INC.

Content Contributors:
Washington Yu Ying PCS™ - Qianyi (Shirley) Zhang, Pearl Zao He You
Level Learning - Jingyao Qi

Illustrations by: Josh Taira

Leveling classification based on Level Learning standard.
For full description, visit www.levellearning.com

ISBN 978-1-64040-113-6
Simplified Chinese Edition

About Level Learning:
Level Learning provides a literacy focused curriculum specifically designed for K-12 Chinese as a Second Language classrooms. Our program offers 20 levels of specific and detailed objectives, leveled texts and passages, mastery-based online assessment, and analytics to enable data-driven instruction. Level Learning reading curriculum for both literature and informational text emphasize grammar and comprehension skills to help teachers develop confident and independent Chinese language readers. The non-fiction series of books are specifically designed to support our informational text course based on multiple national standards. To learn more about our entire offering, visit www.levellearning.com.

About Washington Yu Ying PCS™:
Washington Yu Ying PCS is a Mandarin English dual language immersion International Baccalaureate (IB) World school. Yu Ying's mission is to inspire and prepare young people to create a better world by challenging them to reach their full potential in a nurturing Chinese/English educational environment. Yu Ying's comprehensive IB, dual immersion curriculum equips students with global competencies for success in the real world. As a leader in immersion education, Yu Ying is determined to advance Chinese language programs and global citizenry education by helping other schools create and strengthen their Chinese programs. For more information, email: products@washingtonyuying.org

城市里有什么?城市里有超市、餐馆和医院。人们的日常生活很方便。

城市里有不同的交通工具。人们可以坐公共汽车去上班。人们可以坐地铁去游玩。

城市里有各种各样的公共设施，比如公园和图书馆。人们可以去公园散步。人们可以去图书馆看书。

城市里有漂亮的花草树木。花草可以美化环境。树木可以净化空气。

你知道吗？这些都是城市设计的一部分。这些都是城市设计师的设计和安排。

很多人在城市里生活。城市设计让生活更方便。城市设计让生活更健康。城市设计让生活更美好。

Glossary

	Pinyin	English Definition
城市	chéng shì	city
超市	chāo shì	supermarket, grocery store
餐馆	cān guǎn	restaurant
医院	yī yuàn	hospital
方便	fāng biàn	convenient
交通工具	jiāo tōng gōng jù	transportation
地铁	dì tiě	subway, metro
各种各样	gè zhǒng gè yàng	various kinds
公共设施	gōng gòng shè shī	public facilities
公园	gōng yuán	park
图书馆	tú shū guǎn	library
漂亮	piào liang	beautiful, pretty
花草树木	huā cǎo shù mù	flowers and trees

	Pinyin	English Definition
美化	měi huà	to beautify
环境	huán jìng	surrounding, environment
净化	jìng huà	purify
空气	kōng qì	air
设计	shè jì	to design, to plan
设计师	shè jì shī	designer
生活	shēng huó	life
更	gèng	more
健康	jiàn kāng	healthy, health

www.ingramcontent.com/pod-product-compliance
Lightning Source LLC
Chambersburg PA
CBHW041227070526
44584CB00001B/124